Native
American
Peoples

NAVAJO

D. L. Birchfield

Gareth Stevens Publishing
A WORLD ALMANAC EDUCATION GROUP COMPANY

Please visit our web site at: www.garethstevens.com
For a free color catalog describing Gareth Stevens Publishing's list of high-quality books
and multimedia programs, call 1-800-542-2595 (USA) or 1-800-387-3178 (Canada).
Gareth Stevens Publishing's fax: (414) 332-3567.

Library of Congress Cataloging-in-Publication Data

Birchfield, D. L., 1948-
    Navajo / by D. L. Birchfield.
      p. cm. — (Native American peoples)
    Summary: A discussion of the history, culture, and contemporary life
of the Navajo Indians.
    Includes bibliographical references and index.
    ISBN 0-8368-3704-5 (lib. bdg.)
    1. Navajo Indians—Juvenile literature. [1. Navajo Indians. 2. Indians
of North America—Southwest, New.] I. Title. II. Series.
E99.N3B538   2003
979.1004'972—dc21   2003045707

First published in 2004 by
Gareth Stevens Publishing
A World Almanac Education Group Company
330 West Olive Street, Suite 100
Milwaukee, WI 53212 USA

Copyright © 2004 by Gareth Stevens Publishing.

Produced by Discovery Books
Project editor: Valerie J. Weber
Designer and page production: Sabine Beaupré
Photo researcher: Rachel Tisdale
Native American consultant: Robert J. Conley, M.A., Former Director of Native American
  Studies at Morningside College and Montana State University
Maps and diagrams: Stefan Chabluk
Gareth Stevens editorial direction: Mark Sachner
Gareth Stevens art direction: Tammy Gruenewald
Gareth Stevens production: Beth Meinholz and Jessica L. Yanke

Photo credits: Corbis: cover, pp. 4 (bottom), 8 (top), 12 (bottom), 13, 14, 15 (both), 16 (top),
19 (both), 21, 23, 25, 26 (top), 27; Native Stock: pp. 5, 12 (top), 16 (bottom), 20, 22, 24
(bottom); North Wind Picture Archives: pp. 6, 7 (both), 24 (top); Peter Newark's American
Pictures: pp. 8 (bottom), 10, 11, 18; AP/Wide World Photos: p. 17.

Printed in the United States of America

1 2 3 4 5 6 7 8 9 07 06 05 04 03

Cover caption: Navajo children at Canyon de Chelly on the Navajo Reservation in Arizona.
People have lived at Canyon de Chelly for two thousand years.

Contents

Words that appear in the glossary are printed in
boldface type the first time they appear in the text.

Origins

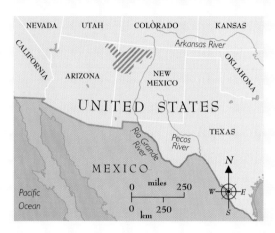

The Navajos settled in what is today New Mexico and Arizona, as shown in red, sometime between A.D. 800 and 1400.

This 1873 photo of a Navajo woman with her child was taken at their home in Canyon de Chelly. Today, Canyon de Chelly is part of a national monument within the Navajo Nation.

Land of the Navajos

The Navajos are a North American Native people, most of whom now live on the Navajo Reservation, which covers large portions of northeastern Arizona, southeastern Utah, and northwestern New Mexico. Numbering more than 200,000, they are the largest reservation-based Indian **nation** in North America. Only the Cherokees have more tribal members, but they are not a reservation-based tribe.

Navajo Origin Story

No one knows exactly how or when Navajos and other Native Americans came to the Americas, but like many ancient cultures, traditional Navajos have long told a story to explain their origins. Navajos believe they have passed through three previous worlds to the present fourth one, which they call the Glittering World. In each of the previous worlds, a lack of harmony among the inhabitants caused them to leave. Living in harmony with the world — and with other Navajos — is an important part of Navajo **culture**.

Monument Valley, a famous landmark in the desert country of the Southwest near the Navajo Reservation. Many Western movies have been filmed in Monument Valley.

New Discoveries

Many scholars have long believed that Navajos and other Indians came to North America from Asia, traveling over a landmass that may have once bridged the Bering Strait during the last Ice Age. Recent discoveries of more ancient Indian sites, some of them at the southern end of South America, have caused scholars to develop different theories. Some people think that perhaps Indians came by boat to South America and walked up to North America. Most scholars agree, however, that Navajos probably came to the Southwest from the far north of present-day Canada and Alaska sometime between A.D. 800 and 1400.

Navajo is thought to be a word from the Zuni Pueblo Indian language, meaning "enemy." The Navajo word for themselves is Dene, meaning "the people." In 1969, the Navajo Tribal Council officially adopted the name "Navajo Nation."

Navajo Words

Here is how some ordinary Navajo words that helped win a war are pronounced. They are from the *Navajo Code Talkers' Dictionary* used in World War II. (See "Navajo Code Talkers" on page 25). Because printing Navajo words properly requires specially shaped letters, only the pronunciations are given.

Pronunciation	English
wol-la-chee	ant
be-la-sana	apple
shush	bear
ba-goshi	cow
chindi	devil
ah-jah	ear
ah-nah	eye
ah-tad	girl

History

Life in the New Land

Navajos have proven to be one of the most marvelously adaptable people in the world. Their adjustment to life in the desert Southwest is an example of that.

Before coming to the Southwest, the Navajos were hunter-gatherers. The men hunted while the women gathered nuts, berries, wild onions, and other food. When the Navajos arrived in the Southwest, their culture was still similar to that of their close relatives, the Apaches. In fact, the early Spanish explorers of the region in the 1500s and 1600s could barely tell Navajos apart from the Apaches, who spoke a similar language.

Pueblo Peoples and the Navajos

Navajos apparently entered the Southwest at about the time of changes in the great Anasazi civilization of cliff dwellers. Partly because of a severe drought in the late 1300s, the Anasazis moved their farming communities to areas with more dependable water supplies near rivers and became known as the Pueblo people.

Those Pueblo people had a great impact on the Navajos, teaching them

This woodcut shows Pueblo Indian farmers in New Mexico watching over their farm fields. The Pueblos remain among the most skillful dry farmers in the world.

farming. Later, when the Spanish introduced sheep and the Pueblos learned to weave blankets and clothing, they passed those skills on to the Navajos.

From the Spanish, the Navajos acquired sheep, soon becoming expert shepherds with huge flocks. All of these new skills — farming, herding, and weaving — brought great changes to the Navajo way of life. By the 1700s, the Navajos were distinctly different from their Apache neighbors.

Navajos learned from the Pueblos that before wool can be woven into rugs on a **loom**, it must first be spun into wool thread.

Anasazi Ruins

In Navajo and Apache culture, all things having to do with the dead are avoided, so Navajos did not disturb the magnificent cliff palaces the Anasazi people had left behind. They left them in the same condition as when the Anasazi people had walked away from them.

This Anasazi cliff village, at the Navajo National Monument, was built sometime between the years 1250 and 1300.

Those spectacular ruins would have been available for scientific study if the Americans who discovered them in the late nineteenth century had not **looted** them of their pottery and virtually everything else that could be carried away. Scientists in the twentieth century were left to dig in the trash heaps of the Anasazis to try to learn about them.

Edward S. Curtis took this photo of Navajos, calling it *Out of the Darkness.* Curtis was the most famous photographer of Native Americans of the late nineteenth and early twentieth centuries, taking thousands of pictures documenting Native life.

Conflict with the Colonizers

By the late 1500s, the Spanish had conquered much of Mexico, but the Navajos, in today's northwestern New Mexico, were too far away from areas of Spanish exploration to be much affected by it. When the Spanish began settling in New Mexico in 1598, however, Navajos soon began to feel their impact.

Throughout the 1600s and 1700s, the Spanish made slave raids against the Navajos, stealing the women and children and killing the men. To meet this threat, the Navajos stole horses from the Spanish and became expert horsemen. By the late 1600s, Navajos themselves were raiding Spanish ranches, stealing their horses, sheep, and cattle, and making Spanish attacks against them more difficult.

This photo of a Navajo man was taken in about 1880. Navajos speak a southern Athabascan language, part of the large Dene language family in North America.

The Spanish never conquered the Navajos. When, however, the United States defeated Mexico in a war in 1848 and acquired New Mexico and Arizona as territories, Navajo life changed dramatically. Americans soon built forts in Navajo country, and settlers began pouring into the Southwest. The Navajos, a proud, freedom-loving people, soon found themselves in conflict with a great military power, one that was determined to force its will on Native people.

Destroying a Homeland

Conflicts with the Americans soon arose over grazing rights. The soldiers at the forts seized land for their animals to graze on around their forts. This pushed some Navajos off their land; when the Indians stood up for themselves, fighting broke out.

Different People, Different Attitudes

It is better to feed the Indians, than to fight them.

William Carr Lane, Governor of New Mexico Territory, 1852

Chastisement [of the Navajos] must be more severe; they must be well punished and thoroughly humbled.

James L. Collins, New Mexico Indian Superintendent, 1859

An Indian is a more watchful and a more wary animal than a deer. He must be hunted with skill.

U.S. Brigadier General James H. Carleton, 1863

A Horse Race Becomes a Massacre

In 1861, about five hundred Navajos gathered for a horse race with the soldiers at Fort Canby in Navajo country. The soldiers cheated by cutting the reins of the Navajo horses, causing them to break during the race. When the Navajos demanded their money back, the soldiers attacked them, killing about forty Navajos. As U.S. Army Captain Nicholas Hodt described the scene at the time:

"The Navajos, squaws [women], and children ran in all directions and were shot and bayoneted. I succeeded in forming about twenty men. . . . I then marched out to the east side of the post; there I saw a soldier murdering two little children and a woman. I halloed immediately to the soldier to stop. He looked up, but did not obey my order."

An 1845 photo of Kit Carson, who led a devastating U.S. Army operation against the Navajos in the 1860s. The government encouraged civilians and other Indians to raid the Navajo homeland during this campaign.

To make matters worse, the United States was soon torn apart by its own **Civil War**. With Americans from the North and South slaughtering each other by the hundreds of thousands in brutal battles, the value of any life seemed cheap. American attitudes toward Indians hardened as well.

The U.S. Army decided to end Navajo resistance by destroying their homeland. That job was given to Colonel Kit Carson, who disagreed with the policy but carried it out anyway. In 1863, Colonel Carson led an army through the Navajo homeland, burning houses, destroying crops, killing sheep and horses, and even chopping down fruit trees.

A Long Walk to Death

By 1864, several thousand Navajos had fled to remote areas farther west, while about eight thousand starving Navajos had surrendered to the U.S. Army. They were forced to walk about 300 miles (480 kilometers), all the way across New Mexico, to the Bosque Redondo prison camp in the "Navajo Long Walk."

The Navajos were kept prisoners at Bosque Redondo, under terrible conditions, until 1868, when they were finally allowed to **negotiate** their only **treaty** with the U.S. government. The treaty allowed them to return to their homeland, but by that time, many had died of disease in the prison camp.

The Congress of the Confederate States has passed a law declaring **extermination** of all hostile Indians. You will therefore use all means to persuade the Apaches or any tribe to come in for the purpose of making peace, and when you get them together, kill all the grown Indians and take the children prisoners and sell them to **defray** the expense of killing the Indians.

Lieutenant Colonel John Robert Baker, Confederate Civil War commander in Arizona and New Mexico, 1862

An 1874 photo of Manuelito (1818–1894). A famous Navajo leader, he signed the Navajo treaty with the United States in 1868.

The surviving Navajos walked back to their destroyed homeland a defeated people. They would never again be at war with the Americans.

Reservation Life

When the Navajos returned home to northwestern New Mexico from Bosque Redondo in 1868, the U.S. government provided them with sheep to begin rebuilding their flocks and with food to support them for ten years. However, the treaty of 1868 reduced Navajo Nation land to 10 percent of what it once was. Over the next few decades, the United States increased the size of the reservation several times, but it remains much smaller than the old homeland.

Navajo students in the Carlisle Indian School Library. This off-reservation boarding school was located in Pennsylvania, all the way across the continent from the Navajo homeland.

Forced Changes

One of the cruelest parts of reservation life was forcing Navajo children to attend boarding schools far from home. The boarding schools tried to turn Navajo children into white people, forcing them to learn the Christian religion and speak English.

The children had to do all the labor at the schools — the cleaning, cooking, and farming that provided the food. In the 1930s, day schools on the reservation began replacing the boarding schools, and Navajo children were able to live at home while attending school.

Navajos had never had a centralized, national government. After oil was discovered on the

Drilling for oil on the Navajo Reservation in 1958, these workers add a drill stem section to a pipe. Payments for mineral leases help support the tribal government.

A tribal council meeting near Window Rock on the Navajo Reservation in Arizona in January 1938. Like many Native nations, the Navajos were forced to create a centralized government by the United States.

reservation in 1921, however, the U.S. government forced them to form a government because it needed one to sign oil **leases**.

A Deadly Discovery

In the 1950s, uranium was discovered on the reservation. The Navajos mined the deadly **radioactive** material, which is used to make atomic bombs, but were not told about its health risks. Many became ill and died of cancer. In 1984, the U.S. government provided money to begin cleaning up the uranium poisoning on the reservation and in 1990 paid money to the surviving Navajo victims of radiation poisoning.

Navajo Stock Reduction

In the 1930s, when Lake Meade, the main water supply for southern California, began filling up with silt, the government blamed it on overgrazing by livestock on the nearby Navajo Reservation. The U.S. government shot hundreds of thousands of sheep, goats, and horses, leaving their bodies to rot and the Navajos in poverty. Scientists later found that silting in Lake Meade had nothing to do with Navajo livestock grazing.

Traditional Way of Life

Traditional Lifestyles

Navajo families are matriarchal, meaning that a woman, usually the grandmother, is the head of the household. Men who marry her daughters become part of the household. When a son marries, he goes to live with his wife's family. Navajo girls grow up learning that they will one day be responsible for leading their family.

During the nineteenth century, Navajos developed distinctive styles of clothing. Women favored colorful blouses and skirts, while men wore jeans, boots, and colorful shirts. A black hat became very popular for men. Both men and women wore silver

This family stands outside their hogan near the south rim of the Grand Canyon. The photo was taken early in the twentieth century.

and turquoise jewelry, a distinctive Navajo tradition that is still very popular.

Made of wood, the typical traditional Navajo house is called a hogan. A hole in the center of the roof allows smoke to escape from the cooking fire. The doorway always faces the rising sun in the east. Navajos typically build a hogan in a valley for their winter home and another one near their mountain pastures for a summer home.

Navajo Silversmithing

Navajos first learned how to make jewelry out of silver from a Mexican silversmith at Fort Defiance, a U.S. Army outpost built in the middle of the nineteenth century in Navajo country. Requiring great skill in hammering and shaping the precious metal, silversmithing is a delicate art. Navajos later added beautiful turquoise stones to create a distinctive jewelry prized by collectors all over the world.

Above: A woman displays her turquoise jewelry at the Navajo Nation Parade. Tourists also buy Navajo turquoise jewelry, adding income to the Navajo economy. *Right:* This silver belt buckle was made by pouring melted metal into a sand mold.

Navajo Weaving

Navajo women first learned how to weave wool from the Pueblo Indians. Working with the Spanish merino sheep wool, they soon began fashioning some of the most beautiful blankets in the world.

This weaver is carding wool, making the wool strands all lie in one direction. She is sitting inside a trading post while working at her task.

This photo, taken sometime during the first half of the twentieth century, shows women weaving blankets from wool on outdoor looms near their home. The outdoors provided more coolness and light for their work than their hogan.

Many families live outside during the summers since the Navajo homeland is mostly desert. People cook and sleep outside, and women set up their weaving looms outdoors, under a pole structure with a roof made of brush to provide shade. Girls learn how to weave from their mother, grandmother, and aunts.

Life with Sheep

The Navajo homeland proved nearly perfect for raising sheep, which provided Navajo families with food (**mutton** stew is a favorite) and fine wool for weaving blankets and clothing. It's an occupation the entire family can participate in, with men and children tending flocks and women weaving, cooking, and maintaining the household.

In the late nineteenth century, trading post operators began selling Navajo blankets, putting them in catalogs that soon made them famous. Today, Navajo weavers offer their blankets each year at a famous sale at Crownpoint, New Mexico, that brings buyers and collectors from all over the world.

Many Navajo boys and girls of all ages spend their summers on horseback, helping move sheep to summer pastures in the mountains and then staying there to tend the flocks. In the fall, men and boys hunt deer in the mountains. Women tend the gardens and peach orchards that add vegetables and fruit to the family diet.

In this 1948 photo, a young sheepherder takes the family flock out to graze at Window Rock, on the Navajo Reservation in Arizona.

A Belief in Harmony

Traditional Navajo values place great importance on living in harmony. Learning about living in harmony begins with the Navajo creation story, in which Navajos have fled three previous worlds because life got too far out of balance. To "walk in beauty" with one's surroundings is more important for Navajos than trying to do many other things, like getting rich. Navajos who acquire wealth are expected to share it with their relatives. Bad behavior for a Navajo is "to act like he doesn't have any relatives." Thus, as with most other Indian cultures, individuals are taught from an early age to think about the welfare of the group.

This medicine man, a Navajo singer, wears a traditional necklace. This photo was taken in about 1900 in New Mexico.

Healing Ceremonies

According to tradition, being out of harmony causes illness. When that happens, Navajos consult experts, called hand tremblers or crystal gazers, who can tell the nature of the illness and recommend the right healing ceremony to restore the patient to harmony. A **medicine man**, called a singer, will then conduct the ceremony.

The purpose of a ceremony is to restore the patient to harmony. As an example, one of the most famous ceremonies is the Enemy Way Ceremony for Navajo soldiers returning from war. The ceremony cleanses the soldier of the **contamination** of death and of other evils from fighting.

A Navajo singer shown during a healing ceremony. More than one thousand different sand painting designs are used in the many different kinds of ceremonies; during a lifetime of study, one singer can learn only a few of the ceremonies.

Songs and Sand Paintings

Long, complicated **rituals**, Navajo healing ceremonies last several days and require many people as helpers, singers, and dancers. The principal singers must study for many years to memorize the songs and sand paintings of just one ceremony.

Though there are many different kinds of ceremonies, there are only a small number of singers to perform them. The ceremonies require such long study that few medicine men are able to learn more than one or two. Some ceremonies have been lost when the only singer who knew them died.

A Navajo singer prepares a sand painting on the ground. Making sand paintings requires years of study to learn the many different patterns used in just one ceremony.

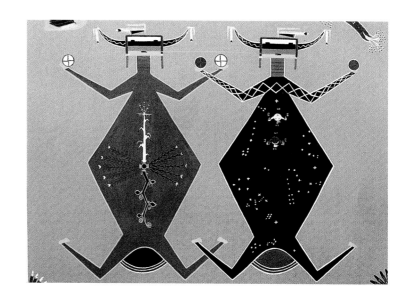

This bold sand painting represents Mother Earth and Father Sky. The image can also be turned upside down.

Hosteen Klah (1867-1937)

In the early twentieth century, Navajo Hosteen Klah became the most famous ceremony singer and weaver. Before becoming the principal singer for one of the longest, most complicated ceremonies, he had to study with older singers for more than twenty-five years to learn all the songs and sand paintings of that ritual. At the end of that nine-day ceremony, he was recognized as one of the greatest singers on the Navajo Reservation. He later caused controversy by using images from sand paintings as patterns in his weaving. Other medicine men thought that sand paintings should not be for public display.

The sand paintings used in the ceremonies are temporary, made on the ground with different colors of sand inside the family hogan. The person being healed sits in the middle of the sand painting, and the illness is transferred to the painting, which is then destroyed.

The Support of the Clan

Other ceremonies celebrate changes in life, such as a girl's **puberty** ceremony, called a *kinaalda*. All of the girl's relatives participate in the celebration of her entry into womanhood, one of the most important events in her life. The kinaalda features songs and dances and lasts for several days.

Ceremonies are very expensive because the family hosting one must feed many people for up to nine days. They must also pay the principal singer a large fee, often in livestock. Deciding to hold a ceremony for someone is a serious decision, requiring the help and support of many relatives. Because so many family members and community members are involved, Navajo ceremonies also help create positive connections between people in the community.

Children get their clan membership from their parents. These clans spread out across the Navajo Nation, giving people extended family across the land. Clan membership carries responsibilities to and for other clan members. Since their traditional culture had no government, clan relationships were — and remain — very important.

This woman is participating in the Spring Snow Ceremony in the mid-1960s. She is in the Luckachuka Mountains on the Navajo Reservation, along the border between Arizona and New Mexico.

Today

Wearing traditional dress and moccasins, the Blue Earth Singers perform on stage in Gallup, New Mexico. Song, poetry, and art remain important in Navajo culture.

Literature and Art

Through literature and art, Navajos may very well have done more than any other tribe in expressing what it means to see the world through the eyes of their culture. Navajo author and storyteller Vee Brown has won awards for her children's versions of traditional Navajo stories. Beautifully illustrated, the books tell of the adventures of Navajo cultural heroes with names like Monster Slayer and Born of Water.

Navajos have also produced many great poets. The songs of the healing ceremonies are works of beautiful poetry. Handed down from **generation** to generation, they were created so long ago that no one knows the names of the people who produced them. These songs were composed before Navajos had a written version of their language, and for many generations the only way to learn them has been to memorize them by studying with a singer, listening to the singer chant the songs.

One modern Navajo who has become famous for expressing what it means to be Navajo in works of poetry is Lucy Tapahonso, a literature professor at the University of Arizona.

This painting by Nelson Tsosie is titled *Silver Horizons*. Tsosie uses images from Navajo life in both his paintings and his sculptures.

Another Navajo professor at the same university who has become famous for his writing is Irwin Morris. His book, *From the Glittering World,* is used in college courses to learn about the Navajo view of the world.

Navajos have also produced some of the most famous Indian painters, including R. C. Gorman, Carl Nelson Gorman, and Paul Apodaca. The Navajo homeland is a strikingly beautiful place that comes alive in the work of these great painters.

Dene College

In 1969, the Navajo people became the first Indian nation to have its own college, originally called Navajo Nation Community College and now called Dene College. Owned and operated by the Navajo Nation, it now has several branch campuses. The main campus, at Tsaile, sits on top of Canyon de Chelly, one of the most beautiful places in North America. Following the lead of the Navajos, about two dozen tribes now have their own colleges.

The famous Window Rock, near the Navajo Nation capital at Window Rock, Arizona.

A farm at Canyon del Muerto on the Navajo Reservation in Arizona. A land of vast spaces, the reservation is so huge that homes can be quite isolated.

The Navajo Nation

When a formal government for the Navajo people was being created in the 1920s, one problem that had to be overcome was the great distances that separated Navajos from one another. Navajos were a rural people, a nation of widely scattered shepherding families. The plan that was adopted created more than one hundred local units called Chapter Houses. Today, the Chapter Houses are still the basic foundation for the Navajo Nation government.

The Navajo Nation Council is the national **legislature** of the Navajo people, who also elect a president to lead the Navajo Nation. The capital of the Navajo

Nation is at Window Rock, in northeastern Arizona. The town is named for a famous rock formation that has a big hole in it, like a window.

The Navajo Nation Tribal Police help to maintain law and order in the nation, and the Navajos have their own court system. The most serious crimes, however, are still investigated by the U.S. Federal Bureau of Investigation (FBI).

The tribe also publishes its own newspaper, *The Navajo Times*. Several radio stations broadcast in the Navajo language, which is spoken by more than 200,000 Natives. With so many speakers, it is in no danger of being lost like so many other Indian languages.

Near the end of World War II, at the Battle of Iwo Jima, one of the most famous battles in U.S. military history, Navajo code talkers were the only Marines who sent radio messages on the battlefield. In 1982, U.S. President Ronald Reagan honored the surviving Navajo code talkers.

Navajo Code Talkers

These Navajo code talkers in World War II were among the first groups of Marines to land on the Japanese-held island of Saipan in the western Pacific Ocean in 1944.

During World War II (1939–1945), more than four hundred Navajos served in the United States Marine Corps, sending radio messages on the battlefield in a secret Navajo-language code. The Marines recruited twenty-nine Navajos to invent the code in 1942. It was so successful that the Japanese were never able to crack it.

A woman demonstrates how to make fry bread over an open fire. Many Navajo women prefer outdoor cooking.

The Navajo Reservation

The Navajo Reservation lies in a high-altitude desert dotted with mountains atop the Colorado Plateau. With cold winters and hot summers, it's a rugged, dry country.

The introduction of automobiles during the early twentieth century ended much of the isolation on the Navajo Reservation. Only the main highways through the reservation are paved, however. Most of the reservation is still lonely backcountry, where horses can get to places cars cannot go.

Much of the reservation still does not have things that most Americans take for granted, like electricity and telephones. People often still use fires to prepare food, and many still depend on their livestock to provide much of that food. Navajo children frequently take long bus rides to school.

The Navajos and Hopis are arguing over a portion of the Navajo Reservation in northeastern Arizona that the two tribes once shared. Some Navajo families have been ordered to leave that land, which has created ongoing problems between the two nations, problems they have difficulty resolving.

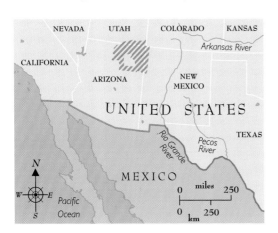

As shown in red, the current boundaries for the Navajo Reservation include land in parts of New Mexico, Arizona, and Utah. The green in the middle represents the Hopi Reservation, which is entirely surrounded by the Navajo Reservation.

Children in a classroom at the Navajo Elementary School on the reservation. Children are taught in Navajo as well as in English.

Looking to the Future

The Navajo Nation has started a number of programs to provide jobs. One is a huge agricultural irrigation project in the San Juan River Valley in New Mexico that is turning desert into cropland. The Navajos, unlike many other tribes in New Mexico and Arizona, have not yet built any **casinos** to provide jobs and income for their people, but they have considered doing that.

Navajos are fortunate to still live in their ancestral homeland, unlike many other Indian peoples who were removed to Indian Territory (now Oklahoma). This has helped them to maintain their culture. They are entering the twenty-first century with confidence and pride — and with more control of their own destiny than many previous generations.

~ Hubbell Trading Post ~

The Hubbell Trading Post is now a National Historic Site on the Navajo Reservation. Trading posts were part general store, part post office, part **pawn shop**, and always a gathering place for Navajos from all around the area. The trading post operators would write letters for Navajos, make loans by taking their turquoise and silver jewelry in pawn, serve as counselors for legal matters, and provide a variety of other services other than just operating a store.

Time Line

A.D. 800 to 1400	Some scholars think Navajos and Apaches arrived in the Southwest from the far north.
1400s and 1500s	Expert farmers, the Pueblo Indians in the Southwest greatly influence the hunting and gathering Navajos.
1600s	Navajos learn how to weave wool from the Pueblo Indians.
early 1600s	Spanish settlers in New Mexico make slave raids against the Navajos; the Navajos fight back by raiding Spanish ranches.
late 1700s	Spanish make historic peace with Comanches and Navajos.
1810–20	Mexican Revolution throws Southwest region into chaos.
1851	U.S. Army builds Fort Defiance in Navajo country, setting off disputes about grazing rights in the area near the fort.
1863	Colonel Kit Carson's U.S. troops destroy Navajo homeland.
1864	Navajo Long Walk: Navajos marched to Bosque Redondo.
1868	First and only U.S. treaty with Navajos allow survivors of Bosque Redondo to return to their homeland.
1882	Hopi Reservation is created within Navajo Reservation.
late 1800s and early 1900s	U.S. government increases size of reservation; sends Navajo children to government boarding schools.
1923	U.S. government forces Navajos to form a national government so oil leases can be made with oil companies.
1930s	Silting of Lake Meade is wrongly blamed on Navajo overgrazing.
1951	U.S. companies discover uranium on Navajo Reservation.
1962	A Navajo-Hopi Joint Use Area is created.
1960s and 1970s	Native protests change government policy toward self-government and education.
1969	Navajo Community College (now Dene College) opens.
1974	Congress tries to force thousands of Navajos to move from Navajo-Hopi Joint Use Area, touching off protests.
1990	Congress provides money to Navajo victims of uranium poisoning.

Glossary

casinos: buildings with slot machines and other gambling games.

chastisement: the act of severely criticizing or punishing someone.

Civil War: 1861 to 1865 war between northern and southern U.S. states.

contamination: the process of becoming unclean or stained.

culture: the arts, beliefs, and customs that make up a people's way of life.

defray: to reduce.

extermination: the killing of everyone or everything.

generation: a group of people born around the same time or one step in the line of descent of a family.

leases: written agreements to rent land or buildings. Mineral leases allow people to have their land mined without giving up actual ownership.

legislature: a group of people elected to make or pass laws.

loom: a frame that holds wool threads to be woven into a blanket or other material.

looted: stolen.

medicine man: a healer and spiritual leader.

mutton: the meat that comes from adult sheep.

nation: people who have their own customs, laws, and land separate from other nations or people.

negotiate: to work with others to come to an agreement.

pawn shop: a store where a person can leave a valuable object in return for a loan of money. The object is left as a promise that the person will return the money.

puberty: the time of physical changes in the human body when a girl becomes a woman or a boy becomes a man.

radioactive: giving off energy in the form of rays. Being near radioactive material can make a person very sick.

rituals: systems of special ceremonies, usually spiritual ones.

treaty: an agreement among two or more nations.

More Resources

Web Sites:

http://www.csulb.edu/projects/ais/dine.html Contains photos of Navajos and their surroundings taken in 1971 with a brief description of Navajo culture.

http://www.weta.org/productions/legacy/weaving/index.html The web site for Woven by the Grandmothers: Nineteenth Century Navajo Textiles has photos and articles about Navajo weavers.

http://www.imagesofarizona.com/dejolie/leroyindex.shtml Navajo photographer LeRoy DeJolie's images of Navajo Nation Fair.

http://www.windows.ucar.edu/tour/link=/mythology/northamerican_culture.html Visit the links to read Navajo stories about the stars, Earth, and various gods.

Videos:

The War against The Indians: The Dispossessed. Madarcy Records, 1995.

500 Nations. Warner Home Video, 1995.

Woven by the Grandmothers: Nineteenth Century Navajo Textiles. Homevision, 1998.

Books:

Armstrong, Nancy M. *Navajo Long Walk.* Scholastic, 1996.

Bial, Raymond. *The Navajos* (Lifeways). Marshall Cavendish, 1999.

Bonvillain, Nancy. *The Navajos: People of the Southwest* (Native Americans). Millbrook Press, 1995.

Roessel, Monty. *Songs from the Loom: A Navajo Girl Grows Up* (We Are Still Here: Native Americans Today). Lerner Publishing, 1995.

Sneve, Virginia Driving Hawk. *The Navajos* (A First Americans Book). Holiday House, 1993.

Woods, Geraldine. *The Navajo* (Watts Library). Franklin Watts, 2002.

Changing with the Times

Navajos have shown great ability to adopt useful things from other people, including farming; raising horses, sheep, and goats; weaving; and making jewelry from silver (silversmithing). Write a short essay about how these things would change the everyday lives of people who had lived mostly by hunting.

You Are There

Pretend you are a newspaper reporter in 1863. Write a short newspaper article about Colonel Kit Carson's war campaign in the Navajo homeland. Now pretend you are a Navajo and write down how you would describe the campaign to other Navajos.

Negotiating a Treaty

Imagine that you are one of the Navajo leaders at Bosque Redondo negotiating the Treaty of 1868. The U.S. government wants to move the Navajos to the Great Plains in Indian Territory (now Oklahoma). Make a list of the arguments you might make for allowing Navajos to return to the Navajo homeland rather than being moved to Indian Territory.

An Art Project

Using markers, paints, crayons, or colored pencils, design your own Navajo blanket or jewelry. Research patterns and designs in other books and on the web sites listed on page 30.

Index